Moses in the Bulrushes

AWARD PUBLICATIONS LIMITED

ISBN 978-1-84135-747-8

Copyright © 2009 Award Publications Limited
℗ 2009 Award Publications Limited

Read by Sophie Aldred
Music composed by Tim King

All rights reserved. No part of this publication may be reproduced or utilized in any form or by any means electronic or mechanical, including photocopying, recording, or by any information storage and retrieval system now known or hereafter invented, without the prior written permission of the publisher.

First published 2009

Published by Award Publications Limited,
The Old Riding School, The Welbeck Estate,
Worksop, Nottinghamshire, S80 3LR

www.awardpublications.co.uk

09 1

Printed in China

Once, long ago, there was a cruel  of Egypt who ordered the death of all Hebrew . The  said that the  must be drowned in the River Nile.

Now, there was one Hebrew  who gave birth to a . She loved him dearly.

"I cannot let the  take my !" she said to her little . "I will hide him."

The brave  managed to hide her  from the  for three months. But soon, her  was too old to hide, and she said to her little , "Bring me some

from the river and I will make a

   for him."

The little  watched her  weave a  for the . It looked like a cradle. "I must make the  watertight so that it will float in the river among the ," her  said.

Early the next morning, when nobody was about, the Hebrew  acted.

Taking the  with her  in it to the river, she put it in among the tall  at the edge of the .

"You must stay close by and keep watch," she told her little .

The little  hid on the bank, not far away from where the  was floating in the  among the .

After a time, the young  from

the 🏛 came to the river to bathe.

As always, some of her faithful  were with her.

When the  spied the 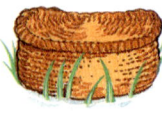 among the , she sent one of her  to fetch it from the .

As soon as the  saw the smiling  lying in the , she said, "He must be one of the Hebrew

 that my father, the , wishes dead!"

The tiny  was so helpless, the  said, "We must save him!"

This was all the little  needed to hear. She ran to the  and asked her if she would like to find a nurse for the .

"I know a kind Hebrew woman who will take good care of the 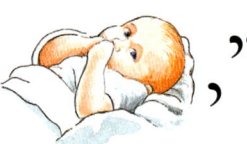,"

the little  said eagerly.

"Bring her to me," said the ,

"and I will hire her to take care of the  in her own home."

The little  ran all the way home to tell her  the wonderful news.

"The daughter of the , the , found our 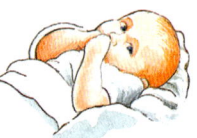," she told

her . "Come at once. She wants to hire you to be his nurse."

The brave  rushed to the river.

Her precious  smiled as she knelt trembling before the .

"You must take good care of this ," the  told her, "until he can come and live in the  with me."

"I will be like a  to him, your Highness," said the new nurse, with a happy smile.

"Call him Moses," the  commanded, "for the word Moses means drawn out of the water."

Moses was now safe from the  of Egypt's fierce , for it soon became known that the  was taking care of him. She did not know that the Hebrew nurse she had hired was really the  of the . Sometimes, the  came with her  to visit the  she had

adopted, and to talk with the

and give her money.

After a few years, the  sent for Moses. In the magnificent  he was treated like a young prince.

He wore the finest clothes, and had lessons with a clever . He was given many  to play with and even a  to ride.

But one of the things Moses liked to

do best was to wander through the wonderful  gardens looking at the   and the  in the sky.

When Moses grew up, he left the court of the 👸 . He was never to return to the 🏛 , for by now he had made an enemy of the 🤴 .

After many years, Moses became the leader of his people, the Hebrews. He promised to lead them from Egypt to a land of their own, where they could live together in peace.